DECISION AT THE JORDAN

DECISION AT THE JORDAN

LEWIS R. WALTON

From time to time the forces of history converge, bringing people to a moment filled with the raw materials of greatness. And I think that is happening today.

It is happening to Adventism.

And it is time to move quickly.

Review and Herald Publishing Association
Washington, D.C. 20012

Copyright © 1982 by the
Review and Herald Publishing Association

Editor: Bobbie Jane Van Dolson
Cover design: Howard Bullard

Texts credited to N.I.V. are from *The Holy Bible: New International Version.* Copyright © 1978 by the New York International Bible Society. Used by permission of Zondervan Bible Publishers.

Library of Congress Cataloging in Publication Data

Walton, Lewis R.
  Decision at the Jordan.

  1. Seventh-day Adventists—Doctrinal and controversial works. I. Title.
BX6154.W327   230'.673   82-7521
ISBN 0-8280-0153-7   AACR2

Printed in U.S.A.

Contents

Prologue	9
Decoded Enemy Orders	15
"The Very Last Deception of Satan . . ."	26
We Would See Jesus	42
The Hour of His Judgment	59
The Real Shaking of Adventism	78
Decision at the Jordan	91

To Jo Ellen and Richie,
my wife and son.

About the Author

With the publication of his stimulating book *Omega*, Lewis Walton, 41, became a sought-after speaker and lecturer. Taking time from a busy law practice, he has now completed *Decision at the Jordan*—his sixth book about Adventism. Between writing, speaking, and practice commitments, he finds relaxation with his family and his hobbies: music (he is an accomplished organist) and aviation (he has a commercial pilot's license).

Walton has received more than a dozen academic awards in the field of law and is listed in *Who's Who in California*.

Prologue

It was evening at the Jordan. Beyond the river rose the mountains of Canaan, ragged in the day's last twilight, a crenelated wall guarding the eastern approaches to the Promised Land. For forty years the people of God had wandered in one of the world's harshest deserts, only a few days' march from the mountain breezes of home, their way blocked by disobedience and unbelief. Now, at last, God had led them to the banks of the Jordan.

Not far distant, perhaps five or six miles as a bird might fly, lay the city of Jericho, one of its wallside windows marked by a mysterious scarlet cord—mute evidence that even honesthearted "heathen" could recognize the message on the wind. To friend and foe alike it was obvious that something great was about to happen. It was time for God's people to go home.

And it was time for them to face a test of faith. This time, would they believe? Would they dare to try the impossible simply because God had said that it could be done?

Would they follow the ark of God into the Jordan?

That, I believe, is the issue facing Adventism today. For years we too have wandered in the wilderness of history while the mountains of home lay distant only a few days' march. We have come close to the very portals of the Promised Land, so near that at one time the latter rain began to fall. Sometimes we too have played with disobedience and unbelief when we should have been entering heaven. But I believe a unique opportunity has come to change all that. I think that God has brought us to the banks of the Jordan. I think that it is time for us to go home.

Why?

Because everywhere I look, I see scarlet cords hanging from the windows of the world.

Listen for a moment to what the world is saying. In Michigan, a former Secretary of the Treasury tells his audience that "it is later than you think. . . . Financial collapse is probable within this century unless the trend is quickly reversed. If collapse does occur, the United States will, in my opinion, simultaneously turn into an economic dictatorship." Should that happen, he warns that there would be "popular demand for a takeover of the major means of production by the state. Legal precedent and ideological justification exist. It would take little to accomplish this transition."

PROLOGUE

In secluded areas across America, bands of armed men dressed in combat fatigues patrol the woodlands for days at a time, learning how to fire weapons, eat freeze-dried food, and read topographic maps. They are not radical commandos bent on changing the status quo. They are people you would probably consider pillars of any community: bankers, corporate officers, physicians—the advance guard of a great host of nervous people, frightened of the future and wondering how to prepare.

And at Harvard University, an Eastern European émigré, with the haunted eyes of someone who has known the inside of a labor camp, tells his electrified audience that "the fight for our planet, physical and spiritual, a fight of cosmic proportions, is not a vague matter of the future; it has already started. The forces of evil have begun their decisive offensive. You can feel their pressure, yet your screens and publications are full of prescribed smiles and raised glasses. What is the joy about?"

Scarlet ribbons, hung out by people who sense what we have always known: that human history is closing, and that somehow we must prepare.

But the greatest proof of all comes from within Adventism. Never within recent memory have so many Adventists been so concerned, so deeply involved, so ready to act. Across the church there is an awakening, like the first awareness of coming crisis. Thousands of Adventists seem to sense that the end is near, that what they do must be done quickly.

I believe that within the past few years General Lucifer has made one of the major tactical errors of his career. He has shot at Adventism, and he has missed. True, his incoming fire has been unpleasant. But the ship is still afloat. And the very attacks that have drawn the world's attention to Ellen White, the sanctuary, and the Sabbath have caused thousands of Adventists to rediscover for themselves truths they otherwise might have taken for granted. In short, I think we have come to a golden moment, filled with enough determination and energy to finish the work of God.

We are at the banks of the Jordan. Heaven is within our grasp. And we too face a decision: will we follow the ark of God through history's last obstacle? Will we stay with the Advent message?

DECISION AT THE JORDAN

1

Decoded Enemy Orders

On a spring day in 1943 the commanding officer of a Japanese destroyer flotilla climbed the boarding ramp of the battleship *Musashi*, announced himself, and then requested an audience with Admiral Yamamoto. To his astonishment, the officer of the deck looked at him as though his request made no sense at all. Embarrassed moments passed; finally the deck officer regained his composure and asked the visitor to follow him through the labyrinth of passageways and ladders that led to the flag officer's quarters. There, for the first time, the visitor learned that something had gone tragically wrong. Inside Admiral Yamamoto's dimly lighted cabin was a long table, on which were arranged seven coffins, wreathed in incense. Admiral Yama-

DECISION AT THE JORDAN

moto, supreme commander of the navy, was dead.

A few days earlier the admiral had decided to visit Japanese installations in the Solomon Islands. Militarily, it was probably a wise decision. The fighting around Guadalcanal was approaching a climactic phase. The outcome of the war might hinge on what happened along this gemlike chain of tropical islands, and Yamamoto made characteristically thorough plans for his tour. A detailed itinerary was encoded and sent by radio to every Japanese base, thus enabling each one to give the admiral all necessary assistance. That too was militarily correct. Nothing that Yamamoto had done was technically wrong; yet all this was leading him straight into tragedy.

For, unknown to the high command in Tokyo, the Americans had laboriously reconstructed the Japanese code machine and had broken the code. As Yamamoto's secret message went out, American communications officers were also listening, taking down details that would vitally affect the course of World War II.

Not long afterward, on an April day, a young fighter pilot by the name of Tom Lanphier climbed into his P-38, started the engines, and taxied onto the active runway at Guadalcanal. For several hours his squadron bored northwestward, scanning the sky for the first glimpse of Yamamoto's flight, and near the island of Bougainville they saw his planes. Throttles and propellers were adjusted, arming switches went to the "on" position, and the American fighters peeled into a firing turn, Lanphier squeezing out bullets at the speck that was growing in his gunsight.

DECODED ENEMY ORDERS

And for a superb Japanese pilot there was the agony of a plane no longer responding to control, a right wing coming off, and a windscreen filled with jungle just before the blackness. The supreme commander of the Japanese Navy was dead.

Why?

Simply because an enemy had decoded his operation order.

Therein lies a lesson for Christians of every race who can see in one man's tragedy a lesson with deep spiritual overtones. For we too have a decoded enemy operation order. It is readily available to nearly every Adventist. It describes exactly how Lucifer intends to attack our church, our faith, and our personal hope for eternal life. It tells what he thinks are Adventism's strong points and weak points. It discloses which persons will be his special targets. It reveals *how* he intends to attack, and *where*. In short, it is a complete, decoded description, of a strategy meeting at the supreme command of the forces of darkness.

And we have the enormous advantage of knowing Lucifer's battle plan in advance!

The exact time is not known. The place can only be located as somewhere on or near Planet Earth. But there can be no doubt about the meeting. For we have the transcript of the proceedings.

Somewhere, sometime after the formation of Adventism, General Lucifer and his high command held a strategy meeting in which they planned how to destroy God's church. An account of that meeting has been given for our information:

"As the people of God approach the perils of the last days, Satan holds earnest consultation with his angels as to the most successful plan of overthrowing their faith. . . . He directs his angels to lay their snares especially for those who are looking for the second advent of Christ and endeavoring to keep all the commandments of God.

"Says the great deceiver: 'We must watch those who are calling the attention of the people to the Sabbath of Jehovah; . . . the same light which reveals the true Sabbath reveals also the ministration of Christ in the heavenly sanctuary.'" [1]

However confused one may become as to the importance of such truths as the law and the sanctuary, it is interesting to note that there is no confusion at all on the part of Lucifer. Speaking with his fallen angels, he lists his strategic objectives. Notice the list of his priorities: the prophetic urgency of Christ's coming, the commandments of God, and the sanctuary. As Satan continues speaking, we gain a chilling insight into his plans for assaulting these strong points of Adventism.

" 'I will influence popular ministers to turn the attention of their hearers from the commandments of God. That which the Scriptures declare to be a perfect law of liberty shall be represented as a yoke of bondage.' " [2]

Not long ago a magazine crossed my desk. In it a writer explained at great length why the law of God is now supposedly a restrictive antique out of another era, its usefulness long past—a yoke of bondage in a jet-age world. The Sabbath, he declared, destroys the liberty of the gospel. Not particularly strange language, perhaps; Adventists have heard it from their Protestant friends for decades. But this paper was written by a man who

DECODED ENEMY ORDERS

once claimed to rejoice in the third angel's message. And I thought, How closely all this follows the script of a decoded enemy operation order in which the ultimate objective is the destruction of Adventism!

In war there are two types of objectives. One is strategic—the enemy capital, for example, representing major victory. The others are tactical, the smaller objectives along the road toward victory. As we read on in this fascinating document, notice how Lucifer begins to mix the two. His great objectives remain, but woven into his thinking are also the methods by which he hopes to destroy truth.

And the first one he lists is working through ministers!

" 'I will influence popular ministers to turn the attention of their hearers from the commandments of God. . . . The people accept their ministers' explanations of Scripture and do not investigate for themselves. *Therefore, by working through the ministers, I can control the people according to my will.*' " [3]

Satan also plans to use important secular minds. " 'We will enlist great men and worldly-wise men upon our side, and induce those in authority to carry out our purposes.' " [4] How? By creating legislation that the majority will view as desirable, but that cannot be obeyed by those who accept the authority of the law of God.

Perhaps the best description of the scene is this:

"Those who honor the Bible Sabbath will be denounced as enemies of law and order, as breaking down the moral restraints of society, causing anarchy and corruption, and calling down the judgments of God upon the earth. . . . In legislative halls and courts of justice, commandment keepers will be misrepresented and condemned. A false coloring will be given to their words; the worst construction will be put upon their motives. . . . Rulers and legislators, in order to secure public favor, will yield to the popular demand for a law enforcing Sunday observance."[5]

It is a brilliant tactic. Adventists, cast in the role of moralists because of their concern with God's law, are suddenly made to seem immoral. The lawkeepers seem to become the lawbreakers. The Sabbath, a sign of divine sanctification, seems instead to symbolize lawlessness. It is the sort of scenario in which, if the issues are serious enough, people can become almost uncontrollably angry.

Before ordering a full-scale assault, however, Satan resorts to a time-honored military tactic. He attempts to soften up his enemy by attacks from within.

" 'Before proceeding to these extreme measures, we must exert all our wisdom and subtlety to deceive and ensnare those who honor the true Sabbath. We can separate many from Christ by worldliness, lust, and pride. They may think themselves safe because they believe the truth, but indulgence of appetite or the lower passions, which will confuse judgment and destroy discrimination, will cause their fall.' "[6]

Today one sometimes hears the suggestion that Adventism, with its unique standards of conduct, health, even dress, somehow separates the believer from Christ. Notice that once again there is no confusion about that on the part of Satan. Through seemingly little things, sometimes questioned as being "unessential to salvation," he readily recognizes the opportunity to rob God's people of judgment and discrimination—perhaps the two human qualities most vital as they approach the masterful deceptions of the end of time.

Stop a moment and analyze what is happening here. Every time Lucifer speaks, the front widens, the war grows larger. He begins by attacking the Sabbath, the Second Coming, the sanctuary. He speaks again, and attempts to draw "popular ministers" into his war plan. Next he targets legislators and civic leaders. Now he reaches into the personal lives of God's people, looking for soft spots through which the forces of darkness can penetrate.

And he has only begun!

His next field of attack is money and property. "'Go, make the possessors of lands and money drunk with the cares of this life. . . . Keep the money in our own ranks. . . . Make them care more for money than for the upbuilding of Christ's kingdom. . . .

"'Through those that have a form of godliness but know not the power, we can gain many who would otherwise do us harm. Lovers of pleasure more than lovers of God will be our most effective helpers. Those of this class who are apt and intelligent will serve as decoys to draw others into our snares.'"[7]

That fateful statement is worth comment. Throughout the history of the church, Lucifer has always made a point of going after the brightest and the best, the very ones God's cause can least afford to lose. They represent the ultimate human prize.

DECISION AT THE JORDAN

Their loss would cost the work of God dearly; their example would drag out others who are inclined to follow natural leaders. And as we shall see, this tactic has been spectacularly successful, even in Adventism.

Now let's resume listening to Lucifer's plan. " 'Those of this class who are apt and intelligent will serve as decoys to draw others into our snares. Many will not fear their influence, because they profess the same faith. We will thus lead them to conclude that the requirements of Christ are less strict than they once believed, and that by conformity to the world they would exert a greater influence with worldlings. *Thus they will separate from Christ;* then they will have no strength to resist our power, and *erelong they will be ready to ridicule their former zeal and devotion.'* " [8]

" 'Thus they will separate from Christ.' " How? Not by surrendering to the objective standard of His law. Instead, separation comes when the people of God become convinced that the requirements of Christ are "less strict than they once believed"! And what follows? Ridicule of their former zeal and devotion.

This is almost too real. This is not the outdated opinion of a little lady speaking to yesterday. This is happening.

And now the commander in chief of the forces of darkness reveals what may be the most chilling plan of all: he will have his agents at Adventist meetings, offering such a persuasive mixture of truth and error that people will no longer believe the plainest principles of Adventism. " 'We must be present at all their gatherings. . . .

" 'I will have upon the ground, as my agents,

DECODED ENEMY ORDERS

men holding false doctrines mingled with just enough truth to deceive souls. I will also have unbelieving ones present who will express doubts in regard to the Lord's messages of warning to His church. Should the people *read and believe* these admonitions, we could have little hope of overcoming them. But if we can divert their attention from these warnings, they will remain ignorant of our power and cunning, and *we shall secure them in our ranks at last.*'"[9]

(Notice that the enemy says "'read *and* believe.'" Some people read but do not believe. Others believe but don't read. Both types are prime candidates for trouble.)

And there you have it, a plan that begins with attack on Adventism's major doctrines and ends with enemy agents in the meetings of the church, sowing seeds of doubt about God's truth and about His messenger. The result? "'Distraction and division.'"[10] A more complete blueprint for attacking Adventism could hardly be given.

Farfetched? We could wish it were. But this is not just academic discussion. This battle plan has already been used against God's church with brilliant military precision and with such success that the result was like a collision between a ship and an iceberg!

The year was 1900. Across the world there was a little time of relative peace, in which, with a few exceptions, the gospel could go anywhere. In America the economy was rebounding into such a soaring prosperity that even jaded newspaper editors exclaimed in surprise. Everywhere doors seemed to be opening for the work of God. If His

DECISION AT THE JORDAN

people followed His counsel, there was no way that they could lose the battle—and there was no way that Lucifer could win.

Now watch the enemy commander turn that situation around so that in just a half-dozen years God's people are in confusion, their greatest institution as good as gone, and their world mission temporarily crippled. Contrary to the Lord's advice, His people have colonized in Battle Creek. Institutions that should have been kept small, according to God's instruction, have grown until they are several times too large. This creates other problems. Workers begin to lose their sense of mission. Around the great Battle Creek Sanitarium coalesces a core of bright, articulate intellectuals who are trained in theology and medicine and who beneath a veneer of professed loyalty actually have little use for either Ellen White or the leadership of the General Conference. Out of this atmosphere emerges such a deep doctrinal heresy that, Ellen White warns, it could destroy the whole rationale for Christianity. And one of the features of this heresy, if one examines it analytically, is an attack upon the truth of the sanctuary.

Against God's express advice (and the vote of church leadership), that very heresy is accepted for printing on denominational presses. And within one tragic year Adventism loses by fire both its major medical institution and its publishing house!

Hard on the heels of these crises comes round two of the devil's counterattacks. A young evangelist named Ballenger, deeply bewildered on the subject of the sanctuary, spreads his confusion with evangelistic gusto. It is a time filled with tragic

DECODED ENEMY ORDERS

might-have-beens. While the last moments of sunlit peace dribble away, a time during which the gospel might have gone in relative ease and prosperity, God's people are confronted with a conflict that seems to threaten the very survival of basic Adventism. In the midst of that crisis Ellen White reaches out, prophetlike, with a symbol to show how deep the danger is. The church is challenged by the "alpha" of deadly heresies, she warns. And then she sounds a warning for the future.

This is not the last time God's church will face such a challenge.

Somewhere in the future, omega will come.

And she "trembles" for our people.[11]

Out of that era—and out of Lucifer's astonishing battle plan—comes an issue facing Adventism today: will we let it happen again?

---

[1] *Testimonies to Ministers*, p. 472.
[2] *Ibid.*, pp. 472, 473.
[3] *Ibid.* (Italics supplied.)
[4] *Ibid.*, p. 473.
[5] *The Great Controversy*, p. 592.
[6] *Testimonies to Ministers*, p. 473.
[7] *Ibid.*, p. 474.
[8] *Ibid.* (Italics supplied.)
[9] *Ibid.*, pp. 474, 475. (Italics supplied.)
[10] *Ibid.*, p. 475.
[11] *Selected Messages*, book 1, p. 203.

2

"The Very Last Deception of Satan . . ."

Toward the end of Satan's battle order he covers a point that should be of deepest interest to Seventh-day Adventists today. He plans an attack on the Spirit of Prophecy.

In so doing he is merely employing an ancient (and highly successful) military tactic: wherever possible, interrupt the enemy's communications network. If you can once trick your adversary into disbelieving messages from headquarters, you have gained an advantage that may mean your victory.

Now put that in the setting of the church. We have entered a phase of history in which, Christ warned, even the "very elect" are liable to be deceived. Nothing could be more important to us than communication from Heaven. For us, that vital

"THE VERY LAST DECEPTION . . ."

communications link is the gift of prophecy. And if the enemy can cause us to distrust God's present-day messages, then he will have begun a process that logically leads to distrust of the Bible, as well.

There is a second reason why Adventists should watch for this development with more than casual interest: this kind of attack will be Satan's "last great deception." In other words, when it happens, time is getting very, very short.

And it is happening today!

What I am about to say I intend to say plainly: I believe the enemy has begun the final offensive of the war. I believe we will soon see Adventism attacked over such a broad front that incoming fire will seem to come from every direction. And I think the assault has already commenced—opened with an attack on the Spirit of Prophecy.

Let's talk, then, about some of the current onslaughts being made against Ellen White, and see whether they reflect a quality of reasoning upon which you would care to hazard your eternal salvation.

1. Plagiarism. The wisest man in history said it best. "What has been will be again, what has been done will be done again; there is nothing new under the sun" (Eccl. 1:9, N.I.V.). That applies to the Spirit of Prophecy in two ways. First, it helps to explain why concepts, ideas, and even language tend to repeat themselves. Second, it speaks volumes about those who would attack Ellen White because of her use of existing literary sources. Let me explain.

Go back for a moment to the year 1887. For Adventism it is a historic and potentially victorious time. In 1887 the Lord is preparing to come—if His

DECISION AT THE JORDAN

people can grasp and apply a magnificent message that will be brought by two young men in Minneapolis the following year. Just a few months before this happens, one of Adventism's brightest ministers—a man named D. M. Canright, legendary for his speaking and debating ability—leaves the faith and becomes one of the church's most articulate foes. He begins at once writing a book called *Seventh-day Adventism Renounced*, which is published in 1889, the very year in which God's timetable provides for the latter rain, an awakened church, and a rapidly finishing work.

And one of Canright's major attacks is that Adventism's prophet, Mrs. E. G. White, is a "plagiarist."

Listen for a moment to the words of Canright. " 'The Bible and the Bible Only, as a Rule of Faith and Practice,' is the Protestant watchword for which saints have fought and martyrs died. . . .

"Seventh Day Adventists have the Bible and—and—something else—Mrs. White's revelations to interpret it."[1]

If that language sounds familiar to you, it is probably not because you read it in Canright's book. More likely you heard it rather recently, spoken or written by someone who was attacking Ellen White.

Hold that thought for a moment and go to the words of Christ: " 'In the same way you judge others, you will be judged, and with the measure you use, it will be measured to you' " (Matt. 7:2, N.I.V.). Now apply that standard to those criticizing Mrs. White. They say that she is not believable because she used words also used by others. Is it possible that they have fallen into their own trap? Are their words their own? They were also used by

"THE VERY LAST DECEPTION . . ."

Canright. Could not one employ against them the argument they use against Ellen White, and say that she is being attacked by "plagiarists"?

Let's admit the fact that Ellen White, like most serious writers, gratefully used ideas and material already available—and for a much better reason than most. Here was a woman with three years of formal schooling, who had looked beyond the veil and seen life and death, an enormous controversy between cosmic powers, the description of which would have challenged a Ph.D. How does one tell the world about such realities raging just beyond the veil that hides the unseen realm? Why not use the vehicle of history?

Like two railroad tracks, her parallel thoughts travel together. On one she places human history, understandable to nearly everyone because it is familiar. On the other she puts the great, unseen controversy, and shows how every event in human life is a result of forces operating beyond the realm of sight. And thus she makes the deepest concepts plain enough for nearly anyone to grasp, doing so in contemporary language.

Not long ago I heard an address by someone who attempted to discredit Ellen White because of the plagiarism issue. It was larger than anyone had imagined, he asserted. She hadn't used just a few books, she had used nearly a hundred. And at that point I wondered whether the speaker really knew whose case he was trying. The sort of comprehensive research he was accusing her of is what one might expect of a serious scholar. To those who do the kind of exhaustive digging she did, we usually award a graduate academic degree. Why, then,

DECISION AT THE JORDAN

choose in this single instance to make well-rounded research the reason for attack? True, Ellen White had prophetic insight—but God had already instructed her to use existing language, where possible, to describe what she had seen, thus taking advantage of work already done.

There is another question such attackers rarely bother to answer: How did Ellen White know when to disagree with the writers she quoted? Any sophomore can copy; how did this woman know when to differ from Harris or Wylie? And why, in nearly every instance, is the literary quality of her work superior to the sources from which she sometimes took illustrations?

Critics, of course, suggest that Mrs. White's "copying" proves that she did not actually see anything in vision. Otherwise, why not put it in her own words? An interesting incident in her life sheds light on that question. Once she visited Zurich. There is no doubt she was there; that is a simple fact of history, attested to by people who accompanied her. Yet when she described what she had seen in that city, she chose to use the beautiful words of J. A. Wylie, who had written *History of Protestantism*. Why? Perhaps it is time we listened to Ellen White for a change instead of to her critics. Early in her life, according to W. C. White and D. E. Robinson, she was "sorely distressed" because of the difficulty of putting into human language some of the truths that had been shown her. "She was told that in the reading of religious books and journals, she would find precious gems of truth" expressed in language she could use, and that heaven would help her to separate truth from error.[2] In 1904 her son explained

"THE VERY LAST DECEPTION . . ."

by letter that "she has sometimes found it very difficult and laborious to put into language the scenes presented to her" and that she "has sometimes copied sentences and paragraphs, feeling that it was her privilege to utilize the correct statements of other writers."[3]

And perhaps, in a way overlooked by her critics, that was indeed her privilege! One spring day just before the Passover, Christ sent two disciples on an errand. " 'Go to the village ahead of you, and at once you will find a donkey tied there, with her colt by her. Untie them and bring them to me.' " If anyone challenged them, they were to utter one simple reply that would immediately resolve the matter: " 'The Lord needs them' " (Matt. 21:2, 3, N.I.V.).

The Lord needs them. The One who had formed the earth itself and lighted the sun in the morning of Creation now needed one of His creatures. No other words were necessary. That settled the issue. And when the Lord of Creation sends any of His children to use something that belongs to Him, He has the perfect right to do so—whether it involves borrowing a donkey or using some literary property that He has given a writer the strength, life and talent to create.

How far will we go in allowing our personal sensibilities to decide what we believe and what we reject? What about the prophet Hosea? To illustrate a point to Israel, God told him to go to the "wrong" section of Jerusalem and find a wife. Shocking? Of course. It was meant to be. To Ellen White the Lord merely gave direction to find and use the words of others. To Hosea He gave the task of finding an unfaithful wife—and then of buying her back when she left him! Reason enough to reject his message, if cultural sensibilities are going to be our criterion for inspiration.

And what about Matthew and Luke, who apparently made use of Mark's Gospel? What about John the revelator's repeated employment of language similar to the non-Biblical book of First Enoch? And Jesus Himself, whose model prayer contains thoughts and words found in the ancient Jewish *Ha-Kaddish?* Will we reject Him, too?

In law school I had the privilege of winning a national award with a legal paper I had written on the concept of "fair use," a doctrine by which the law defines the circumstances in which one writer may properly copy another. The basic rule is that such copying is proper if it is done as part of one's independent research and creative effort. Were this not allowed, no progress could possibly be made in science, history, or basic research, for the first finder of truth would thereby become its owner. Ellen White's use of literary sources falls well within that common-sense doctrine of the law.

Now, lawyerlike, I have saved one of my best witnesses for the last. His name is John Harris—the same John Harris whose beautiful book on the life of Christ Ellen White used at times (a practice for which some would now condemn her). And I quote from that very book:

"Suppose, for example, an inspired prophet were now to appear in the church, to add a supplement to the canonical books—what a Babel of opinions would he find existing on almost every theological subject! and how highly probable is it

"THE VERY LAST DECEPTION . . ."

that his ministry would consist, or seem to consist, in the mere selection and ratification of such of these opinions as accorded with the mind of God. *Absolute originality would be almost impossible.*" There would, in Mr. Harris' opinion, be *"little more, even to a divine messenger, than the office of taking some of these opinions, and impressing them with the seal of heaven."* [4]

The defense rests.

2. Supposed use of J. N. Andrews' work. In attacking truths that are basic and sound, people sometimes grasp at extremely frail straws. Such, it seems to me, is the claim that Ellen White is not believable because some of her writings bear resemblance to the ideas of James White and J. N. Andrews. One might wonder whether such arguments even deserve rebuttal. Adventism began as a scholarly quest by a group of people drawn from different Christian backgrounds and different walks of life. Sometimes entire nights were spent in study and prayer. In the midst of that group was Ellen, a young Christian woman who often could not even understand the theological points in question until the Lord took her into vision and enabled her to grasp the most complex problems with simple clarity. Usually this was done after the others had studied and come to a conclusion.

Under the circumstances it would be incredible if Ellen White's writings did not closely resemble the thinking of other Adventist pioneers. J. N. Andrews was a fine scholar and a part of the beginning of Seventh-day Adventism. His ministry began in 1850, while many new truths were still being researched. These truths were learned through common effort and were held in common, even though Andrews might have been the first spokesman. Far from discrediting Ellen White, her similarity to Andrews ought to reinforce one's faith in a message that could incorporate so many divergent backgrounds and still produce such unity of thought.

And are we to take seriously the argument that Ellen White was a fraud because she happened to agree theologically with her husband?

Such shallow ideas raise an issue quickly recognizable by any trial lawyer. When one's courtroom opponent chooses to attack large issues with trivia, it is obvious to everyone that he really has nothing meaningful to say.

Such, I submit, is the case here.

3. The "shut door." Perhaps no single item has been worn so threadbare as the claim that Ellen White once incorrectly thought that the door of probation had shut for the world after October 22, 1844.

For a time, as a young woman, Ellen Harmon did indeed think that. Later, in December of 1844 she had her first vision in which she saw three groups of people: the living saints who still believed in the October 22 experience, former Millerites who denied the Advent message as a mistake, and a third group, the "wicked world," which God had rejected. For a time she misinterpreted this vision. She incorrectly assumed that the 144,000 referred only to existing Adventists.

Before one triumphantly declares that Ellen White is therefore not inspired, it is well to remember that the same problem faced the Bible prophets. Daniel saw the great vision of the 2300

"THE VERY LAST DECEPTION . . ."

days and confessed that he was "appalled" by it and that it was "beyond understanding." Peter at first struggled to grasp the meaning of a sheet filled with unclean animals. And Ellen White openly admitted that sometimes she did not understand what she had been shown until the Lord gave her the same vision a second time or explained it with another vision.

That seems to have been the case with the "shut door." On January 5, 1849, Mrs. White was shown "that Jesus would not leave the Most Holy Place until every case was decided either for salvation or destruction."[5] While some, by their own decisions, might have closed the door of probation on their own lives, the door obviously remained open for the world at large, a fact that brought added urgency to Adventism's world mission.

And, as Ellen White pointed out, in 1844 doors actually had opened and shut in heaven. The holy place phase of Christ's ministry had ended, and He had begun His final work for mankind beyond the door described in Revelation 3. One door had shut; another had opened; and that fact was one of Adventism's special messages to the world.

Perhaps therein lies the reason why the enemy has made such an issue of this. By causing people to focus on the pioneers' sometimes painful quest for truth (rather than on the truth they ultimately discovered), the enemy can accomplish a clever diversionary tactic. Real issues can thus be masked with spurious ones. It is a tactic Lucifer has used again and again.

4. "The words . . . are my own" "I am as dependent upon the Spirit of the Lord in writing my views as I am in receiving them," Ellen White wrote in 1867, "yet the words I employ in describing what I have seen are my own, unless they be those spoken to me by an angel."[6]

Because she sometimes employed the words of other writers, critics suggest that it was improper for her to claim that the words were "her own." For someone who regularly works with words, that argument has very little merit. Let me explain.

When someone asks an attorney to prepare a will minimizing estate taxes, that person will probably end up with a document filled with language and concepts out of the Internal Revenue Code. The careful lawyer will also consult Revenue Rulings and Regulations, as well as provisions from previous wills that have survived challenge in the U.S. Tax Court. And when he is finished he will say, "Mrs. Jones, *I* have drafted your will."

In the eyes of the law, he most assuredly has drafted that will. He may have used the language of others, but the words have become "his own." And the best proof of that fact is his responsibility in malpractice if "his" will fails to produce the results he had promised.

What was Ellen White saying when she stated that the words were "her own"? Merely that God gave her revelations of truth that she then had to find language to describe. Sometimes her vocabulary was pressed to its limits, and she looked for other language, already in existence, that would capture the panorama of truth she had seen. The words became hers. God had left her with that responsibility.

That was the same method He generally used

"THE VERY LAST DECEPTION . . ."

with Bible writers, many of whom quoted copiously in an effort to describe complex truths. They copied from one another. They copied from non-Biblical writers. They used data from history and court annals. Paul even quoted Greek poets. If we allow our faith in Ellen White's writings to be shaken by such arguments, intellectual honesty will compel us to question the Bible as well.

If this happened, General Lucifer would accomplish exactly what he really wants: a complete breakdown of communications between God's forces and headquarters!

5. Supposed "historical errors." If one disagrees with a book but cannot successfully refute it, he or she may still try to attack the book's credibility by alleging that it is "full of errors." That is an inexpensive shortcut that does not require the persuasive exercise of logic. Instead, it operates on the theory that at least some people will be gullible enough to believe such charges without learning the facts for themselves.

And it presupposes that if the critic appears knowledgeable, many people will be impressed by his arguments. Before one becomes unduly distressed by wordy attacks on Ellen White, it might be well to remember that the world's scholars have a dismal record when it comes to refuting God's truth. Not very long ago supposed experts solemnly assured the world that the book of Daniel was full of errors. They sneered at its reference to a king named Belshazzar, for their research "proved" that no such king ever existed. Some people believed them—until archeologists discovered artifacts that pointed conclusively to his existence!

DECISION AT THE JORDAN

People at the time of Noah may have convinced the world of the physical impossibility of tons of water coming from the sky, for only eight people entered the ark. Other learned men, supposedly expert in the Scriptures, once declared that the sun revolved around the earth—and ordered Galileo to recant when he declared otherwise. Today some Biblical scholars waver when asked about their belief in the Creation story.

Let's look at one example of historical criticism directed at Ellen White. Some critics suggest that *The Great Controversy* is unreliable because of historical errors. Their proof? Ellen White differs from a certain historian as to the year in which John Huss did certain things in the city of Prague. But the critics base their conclusions on a letter written by John Huss that does not even bear a date!

Suppose that Ellen White did make some mistakes regarding history. The truly open-minded person will recognize that even someone who is divinely inspired may, like Daniel, struggle for a while to grasp the full meaning of a massive truth. He or she may grope for words, borrow language. To illustrate a point, the inspired one may even borrow facts from history. If those borrowed facts are later found to contain some errors, should we ignore the larger message because of small mistakes in method? Of course not—unless we disagree with the message itself and are looking for an excuse to throw it out. In the latter case we might gleefully seize upon the most absurd trivia in order to rationalize our disagreement. I suggest that is very much like rejecting directions about the way out of a burning building because the fireman stutters or

"THE VERY LAST DECEPTION . . ."

has warts.

But that sort of reasoning has all too often been employed against Ellen White. Some claim to be troubled because she used literary assistants; they ignore the fact that Peter, Paul, and Jeremiah all seem to have used the same common-sense technique. God chose to reveal truth through human beings who were then free to decide how they could most effectively communicate truth to the world. We can be thankful that He does not constrain His messengers with the same rigid rules that have been suggested by some of their critics.

6. *Sola Scriptura.* One of Satan's most effective techniques has been to discredit one truth by pretending to exalt another. Here is a classic example. Ellen White is attacked by people who claim to want to hear only the Bible, but who reject that portion of the Scriptures that foretells the gift of prophecy in the last days.

Remember that Canright took this approach nearly one hundred years ago. "The Bible and the Bible Only" were words published in 1889 by Dudley Canright, who had left the Adventist Church. He too pretended to exalt the Scriptures while attacking Ellen White, and spent his last years lingering pathetically on the fringes of Adventism, privately admitting that for him it was "too late."[7]

Remember, too, that the Son of God was crucified at the insistence of theologians who rejected His message with the concept of *sola Scriptura*. They had Moses; they had no intention of listening to a Galilean carpenter. And thereby they rejected the Creator Himself.

The expression *sola Scriptura* arose out of the

DECISION AT THE JORDAN

Protestant Reformation. The question then was What is the source of prime authority in matters of faith and practice? For Rome, it was the church. For Protestants, it was the Bible and the Bible alone—not the Bible and tradition. Recognizing that conflict as the origin of the expression *sola Scriptura*, we cannot allow it to split the Bible away from its own doctrine of spiritual gifts. "The Bible and the Bible alone" was never meant to pit Scripture against the gift of prophecy, for both arise from the same Holy Spirit.

Of course, the Bible is the basis for Seventh-day Adventism. The truth of Adventism came out of intense study of the Word of God, and it is still fully supportable out of Scripture. But those who reject the added blessing of the Spirit of Prophecy remind me of an astronomer who claims to be a purist, who insists on information direct from the stars, and who resents the intrusion of an intervening telescope.

And so in the messages of Ellen White we are confronted with an issue that forces a decision. We may not like what she says, but we cannot ignore her.

"All who believe that the Lord has spoken through Sister White, and has given her a message, will be safe from the many delusions that will come in these last days," she wrote in 1906, and earlier she had warned that "one thing is certain: Those Seventh-day Adventists who take their stand under Satan's banner will first give up their faith in the warnings and reproofs contained in the Testimonies of God's Spirit."[8]

Even her attackers unwittingly validate the very

messages they try to discredit, for they fulfill a prediction she made back in 1890.

"The *very last deception of Satan* will be to make of none effect the testimony of the Spirit of God. . . . There will be a hatred kindled against the testimonies which is satanic. The workings of Satan will be to unsettle the faith of the churches in them, for this reason: Satan cannot have so clear a track to bring in his deceptions and bind up souls in his delusions if the warnings and reproofs and counsels of the Spirit of God are heeded."[9]

One of the major tactics in General Lucifer's battle plan is an attack on the Spirit of Prophecy. For him that is an absolute military necessity. And in implementing it he reveals to thoughtful Adventists exactly where they stand in the stream of human history.

"The very last deception . . . "

We are at the Jordan.

Time has almost run out.

And we must decide whether we will stay with the ark or whether the next chapter in the story of God's people will be written by the general of darkness.

---

[1] D. M. Canright, *Seventh-day Adventism Renounced*, 14th ed. (New York: Fleming H. Revell Co., 1889), p. 165.
[2] W. C. White and D. E. Robinson, "Brief Statements Regarding the Writings of Ellen G. White" (Elmshaven office, St. Helena, Calif.: August, 1933), p. 5.
[3] W. C. White to J. J. Gorrell, May 13, 1904.
[4] John Harris, *The Great Teacher*, 2d ed. (Amherst: J. S. and C. Adams, 1836), pp. xxxiii, xxxiv. (Italics supplied.)
[5] *Present Truth*, August, 1849, p. 22.
[6] *Review and Herald*, Oct. 8, 1867, p. 260.
[7] Carrie Johnson, *I Was Canright's Secretary* (Washington, D.C.: Review and Herald Pub. Assn., 1971), p. 135.
[8] *Selected Messages*, book 3, p. 84.
[9] *Ibid.*, book 1, p. 48. (Italics supplied.)

3

We Would See Jesus

It was springtime in Jerusalem—a festive time, filled with preparations for Passover, bright with springtime's flowers. But for Jesus it was already late autumn.[1]

Never had His life seemed so destined for defeat. True, He had brilliantly outclassed the Pharisees, defeating them at the very word games with which they had tried to trap Him.[2] But He had not won their hearts. The highest leadership of His chosen people—the cream of the cream, if one chose to think of it in human terms—not only had rejected Him but would soon murder Him.[3]

Springtime. But there was death on the wind.

And then occurred one of those fleeting vignettes that shines like momentary sunlight through the clouds of gathering storm. Out near the barrier that excluded Gentiles from the Temple court came a request that shattered the gloom. Some Greeks had located one of the disciples, and across the crowded space came words that brightened His heart: "Sir, we would see Jesus" (John 12:21).[4]

Once in a while someone captures the deepest issue in the simplest terms. So it was that day in Jerusalem. In just a few words some unnamed, honest-hearted foreigners had expressed Christianity's greatest opportunity and its greatest challenge.

We would see Jesus. No message on earth could so meet the needs of a world full of people, many of them hungry, some of them frightened, all of them wondering about the unknown future. There was nothing that people needed so badly as to see Jesus, and for most of them, the only hope they'd ever have of seeing Christ was to see Him in some Christian's life.[5]

If Christianity ever really delivered that message, heaven itself was within grasp. The war would soon be over. The message would go like fire in a hayfield. And God's people could go home.[6]

The converse was also true. If people uttered the majestic claims of Christianity and then failed to live that message, humanity's unfulfilled longings would create almost unendurable pressures for something else—Islam, for example. And there would be hordes of cynics, and armies of believers fighting believers, and a world whose disappointment was summarized by Chief Joseph of America's Nez Percé Indian tribe as his people lost their homeland: "It makes my heart sick when I remember all the good words and all the broken promises."[7]

In the years following 1844, Adventists ventured by faith inside heaven's Holy of Holies, where John had once seen the "ark of his covenant" (Rev. 11:19, N.I.V.) and there they discovered a wealth of new truth.[8] Within the ark, they found the ultimate answer to the Greeks' age-old request, the world's best way of showing Jesus. They rediscovered the very transcript of His character, the law of God.[9]

Christians frequently say that Jesus can be revealed to the world simply by showing love. In theory, of course, they are right. Everything about Him—the law included—is the very incarnation of love. But love is an abstract term, and over the centuries humanity had shown a distressing capacity for turning that beautiful abstraction into something distastefully hypocritical. Christian fought Christian for love of country. Homes were broken, and little children left in bewildered loneliness because of a father's (or mother's) new "love." All too often the word seemed to be a cloak, behind which hid a lot of misery. If humanity needed to show love, it also clearly needed some concrete guidance on how that divine blessing was really displayed—something absolute, something beyond the power of human rationalization. To put it briefly, mankind needed law's description of love.

Without law, humanity could not relate objectively to love!

There was nothing strange about that, really. Law was the way God displayed His love every day. The warmth of sunlight. The certainty of seasons. The healing powers of the human body. Every last person on earth, even those in open behavioral rebellion, relied for survival upon divine law: gravity, friction, the life-giving thermodynamics of sunlight. Nearly every religion, however heathen, recognized that there was a role for law. Yet within Christendom one encountered a paradox. People who claimed to be saved by Jesus also claimed to be relieved by Him from obedience to the transcript of His character.

But in Adventism, Christianity was going to have to face that issue head-on. As early as 1844 some Millerite Adventists began rediscovering the Sabbath in the Word of God, thus illustrating in the most emphatic way possible the existence of God's ten commandments. Having already astonished the world with the declaration that judgment had begun, this little group (not yet even an organized church) declared that the law of God was still in effect.

And thus Adventism confronted the world with still another uncomfortable challenge. Love was an amorphous word, one that could be used to hide some remarkable rationalizations. But the law could not be rationalized away—not if a person had an iota of intellectual honesty. It was an absolute. It said what love *did* do and what it did *not* do. When one reached the law, talk ended and action began.

One accepted law or one didn't; it was as simple as that. And the moment anyone tried to make God's law relative, submitting it to the whims of individual judgment, he entered the thorniest patch of confusion ever encountered by the human mind. If the Christian truly believed that law was relative to one's training, background, and social system, then what did he have to say to the convert in Cannibal Valley?

"Congratulations on your baptism, brother. We recognize that your cultural background gives you an ungovernable desire for human flesh. We understand. But to show your gratitude for the freedom of the gospel, please do remember to say the blessing over your victim."

Absurd? Of course. But the best way to unmask a false premise is to demand that it be carried to its logical conclusion. To those who would bend God's law into something less than absolute, that same law poses an unanswerable question. If you are willing to be comfortable with only partial performance, passing off your failure as an excusable result of social background, then which sins are you willing to tolerate? Certainly not the cannibal's; you have already expressed abhorrence at his diet of human flesh. Which sins, then? Only the nice ones indulged by polite society? Verbal cannibalism, for example? Pride? Immorality masquerading as "love"?

Which? Logic demands an answer.

The point should be as obvious as a summer sunrise. Either one accepts God's authority or he doesn't. Either one surrenders to Christ or he doesn't. Through Him, either one lives Christianity or he doesn't. *And God did not call Seventh-day Adventism into being to give the world its best-reasoned theological excuses for failure.*

Paul—who had studied under Gamaliel, and who brought his legal insights into Christian theology—grasped it all in a few excuse-shattering words: "What shall we say, then? Shall we go on sinning so that grace may increase? By no means! We died to sin; how can we live in it any longer?" (Rom. 6:1, 2, N.I.V.). In Revelation the Son of God repeatedly warns His church about the error of the Nicolaitans, a group who seem to have believed that one's moral life did not affect his soul—a doctrine toward which Christ expressed hatred.

"There are many who cry, 'Believe, only believe.' Ask them what you are to believe. Are you to believe the lies forged by Satan against God's holy, just, and good law? God does not use His great and precious grace to make of none effect His law, but to establish His law."[10] Elsewhere she warned of popular religious movements that would pretend to exalt faith while downgrading the only evidence that faith exists, a growing, victorious Christian life. "It is not faith that claims the favor of Heaven without complying with the conditions upon which mercy is to be granted, it is presumption. . . .

"Let none deceive themselves with the belief that they can become holy while willfully violating one of God's requirements. The commission of a known sin silences the witnessing voice of the Spirit and separates the soul from God."[11]

Seldom had Christendom encountered anything quite like this. A group of New England farmers and day laborers were challenging everything that allowed Christianity to live comfortably with its record. They were stripping away every last shred of an excuse for failure in the Christian life. And they were simultaneously confronting people with the awesome thought that for professed believers, final judgment was already underway. If those who professed to love Jesus could catch fire from this message, there was nothing in the world they couldn't do.

"We would see Jesus," the eager strangers had said, and modern Christianity was being given the vehicle for delivering that message. A small group of Bible students was challenging faith to its ultimate: asking from it not excuses for failure, but the victorious life of Christ through continuing surrender to Him. Building on the foundation of faith that claims forgiveness, they saw that faith grows—not into excuses, but into victory. This was something the world deserved to see. This message could shake the world. This message could give even Cannibal Valley the mightiest hope of all: that the gospel meant transformation by the indwelling power of Christ.

And this message threatened Lucifer as nothing had since that awesome day when the Holy Spirit swept through an upper room in old Jerusalem and a handful of people went out to change the world. For this challenge, General Lucifer was prepared to call in every reserve force on earth.

As one looks back at history, it is rather obvious that Satan had seen something like this coming. He understood, far better than did mankind, the import of the great 2300-year prophecy. Somewhere toward the end of that time period God would probably choose to warn the world. He would see people whom He no doubt would equip with at least some of the gifts seen in His followers of old.[12] One of the most probable was the gift of prophecy. From the vantage point of history it would appear that the prophetic gift was considered by Lucifer to be one of his most serious threats and most important targets. Why? Because, like any military general, he recognized that one of his highest priorities was to destroy the enemy's communication system. For God's people, the gift of prophecy is His communication system. Satan could do nothing to hold that gift back should God choose to send it, but he could do something else. He could attack it before it ever arrived. He could preempt it with a counterfeit.

In late September, 1827, just two months before the birth of Ellen Harmon, a young man in rural New York announced that a visitor from heaven had delivered to him a special set of golden plates on which the history of a lost tribe of Israel supposedly was written. With the aid of "magic" spectacles, he claimed to be able to translate the strange symbols to a scribe (who dutifully transcribed his dictation from behind a curtain). His message contained a surprising number of elements that would soon be seen in Adventism: the concept of a last-day remnant of true believers, a vision of world evangelism, some practical ideas for personal and family living, even rules of health. And, of course, the claim that all this resulted from a modern-day prophetic gift.

A number of people were attracted to his message, and in 1830 the group formed a new religious denomination, just a short distance from the New York town where William Miller would soon give his first sermon on prophecy. For the student of history, the timing of that event is fascinating. Just fourteen years before the great Adventist discoveries concerning the sanctuary, a church was formed that emphasized human priesthood and ceremonies in temples built on earth.

Following this historical theme through, one encounters a second fascinating "coincidence." In the 1860s, after Ellen White had received her major vision on health reform, another woman appeared who also claimed insights into Christianity and health. Her name was Mary Baker Eddy, and many of her followers considered her to be divinely inspired.

There was abundant other evidence that Satan was taking the challenge of Adventism very, very seriously. In 1831 a young Englishman named Charles Darwin boarded the H.M.S. *Beagle* and commenced a survey tour of the Pacific Ocean. Upon his return he began to formalize a theory that would attack the very rationale for both the first angel's message and the fourth commandment, each of which relies upon the existence of a creating God. In 1844, Darwin wrote the main outlines for the thesis that would subsequently be published in his book *On the Origin of Species*, thus becoming the father of organic evolution.

Then there were the crises in the political world. In 1848, the year of the first Sabbath Conference, Europe exploded in revolution. France, Italy, and Austria were shaken by the famous Revolutions of 1848. French protesters were shot dead in the streets of Paris, and their bodies were carried through the city in a great open van, illuminated by an eerie torchlight procession. Troops and crowds traded gunfire in Vienna and elsewhere. In the very midst of this turmoil was a young firebrand by the name of Karl Marx, who had recently written a document called the *Communist Manifesto* and whose theories—if ever adopted by national governments—could close great areas of the world to the gospel.

And in America, where Adventism was being organized and financed, there was an inexorable drift toward the divisive catastrophe of civil war!

Religious counterfeits. Evolution. Civil revolt. Communism. General Lucifer was obviously directing his heavy iron at this era, this movement, and the future of the work of God. Everywhere throughout the history of the late 1840s one sees God's movement being met by intense tactical countermeasures, some of them astonishing for their brilliant, long-range implications. But the enemy would soon relearn a lesson that always seemed difficult for him to remember: that attacking God's people frontally was not the way to destroy their effectiveness. When confronted with persecution and discouragement, they had usually responded splendidly, absorbing the enemy's worst attacks while sending the gospel everywhere. If Lucifer really wanted to neutralize the effectiveness of Adventism, he would have to employ a tactic that he had used repeatedly and that was all too often successful. *He would have to attack from within!*

An army may survive intense attack so long as it is in a strongly defensible position and deeply believes in its cause. (Grant learned that lesson expensively in America's Civil War, discovering after many bloody encounters that one simply did not attack Gen. Robert E. Lee when his troops were behind adequate fortifications.) But let division

DECISION AT THE JORDAN

enter the ranks—let people begin to wonder about the rightness of their purpose—and problems rapidly can become very serious. If internal uncertainty continues, the issue can soon go far beyond fulfillment of mission. It can involve survival itself.

In Adventism the enemy recognized some built-in issues that could be used to foment internal confusion. The Sabbath. The sanctuary. The investigative judgment. The law. All were dramatic departures from the main body of Christian theology. Some, such as the Sabbath, cost dearly in employment opportunities and even family ties. And if Satan worked skillfully enough, he just might batter down the believer's defenses with a subtle but deadly question: In the end, was all this really essential for one's salvation?

In making such an attack, Satan had a powerful ally called human nature. For the standards of Adventism, coming out of the sanctuary and the law of God, were foreign to human selfishness.[13] The law demanded from people something better than lip-service Christianity.[14] It was one thing to rejoice in the magnificent gift of eternal life. It was quite another to be told that the gift carried with it the greatest imaginable responsibilities, made even more intense because of ongoing judgment.[15] Real Adventism could not be lived halfway; either one committed everything or one did not, and for those who claimed to believe but who did not really surrender self, Christ had His most scathing rebuke: "'You are lukewarm,'" He said. "'I am about to spit you out of my mouth,'" (Rev. 3:16, N.I.V.).

Adventists had claimed to discover an Elijah

message, a message that began on earth and ended in heaven. Soon, they said, a generation of people would see the face of God. Like Enoch and Elijah, they would enter heaven without going through the grave. The intense challenges and tribulations of the last days would so drive them to dependence on Christ that they would surrender absolutely to Him. People still mortal and still potentially capable of sinning would be so fully surrendered to God that He could rely on them not to change their minds.

Think about that for a moment. God was planning to demonstrate the power of salvation by granting a final judgment of eternal life to men and women who for a little while would remain on earth—still mortal, still living in a world of sin!

No greater privilege could be offered to a human being. For this group of people something fabulous seemed to await in God's tomorrow. In vision, Ellen White saw the temple of God. At its portals, Christ Himself declared, "Only the 144,000 enter this place." [16] Amid the wrenching forces of earth's last moments, some would follow Christ by faith into that temple, finding there His strength to do the impossible. Later, they alone would follow Him there in reality.

That was the prospect Adventism described. "Higher than the highest human thought can reach is God's ideal for His children. Godliness—god-likeness—is the goal to be reached," [17] Ellen White wrote, and elsewhere she made it plain that "there is nothing that Christ desires so much as agents who will represent to the world His Spirit and character." [18]

Thus Adventism reminded both the world and

DECISION AT THE JORDAN

the believer of God's high standard. For His people at the end of time God had a special work that seemed to involve the quality of their lives deeply. To a world living in its last moments they would give the warning of judgment, and through their lives would be shown the character of the Judge. But their work transcended even earth.[19] To the onlooking universe, they would allow God to demonstrate through them that Satan's charge was false—that even at the bitter end of human history, a generation of people could still receive the mighty new covenant promise: " 'I will put my laws in their minds and write them on their hearts,' " (Heb. 8:10, N.I.V.).

And if Lucifer wished to do so, that standard of life could be falsely labeled as "legalism" or "perfectionism."

The charge, of course, was utterly untrue. Adventism was the very antithesis of both. By reminding one of judgment and of law, it underscored as did no other theology humanity's desperate need of a Saviour. It challenged the believer to use the name of Christ not as a cloak to cover cherished wrongs, but as the greatest tool in all creation—indeed, as the power of creation itself.[20] David had grasped this. "*Create* in me a clean heart, O God" (Ps. 51:10). Christianity, after all, claimed to worship a Lord who had emerged from a shattered grave with the mightiest possible proclamation: "All power is given unto me in heaven and in earth" (Matt. 28:18). Power even to repair a human life![21]

"Thou shalt call his name Jesus," the angel had said, "for he shall save his people from their sins" (chap. 1:21). *From* their sins, not *in* them!

Adventism merely proposed to take that promise at face value. Some, even inside the church, might call that perfectionism. But Ellen White clearly said that it was not. No one could claim such a thing, she declared; indeed, the closer one came to Jesus, the more he realized the failure of his past—much as a man being rescued from a well might realize, with each passing foot, just how far he had fallen. He would never claim that "he" had climbed out of the well. Some loving force at the top had drawn him upward. It was not legalism that had lifted him, but a Creator's love. And it was not "perfectionism" for him to rejoice as he was drawn nearer and nearer to glorious sunlight. He was merely hanging on to God's promises by faith. *But he was being lifted!*

That was Christianity.

That was the Advent message.

And *that* was what the world had waited centuries to see.

Some would find in that ideal an apparent contradiction. The gospel was a free gift, was it not? To demand anything of the believer was inconsistent with the nature of a gift. But Christ had already answered that objection in the parable of the pearl of great price. The one who found it had to sell everything in order to have it.[22] Before one could be drawn upward on the cord of faith, he had to leave everything else at the bottom of the well. And that was a sacrifice some were simply unwilling to make.

Some, then, might be attracted by the subtle concept of forensic righteousness—that the gospel merely declares people righteous without the inconvenience of actually overcoming sin. To believe such a teaching they would have to ignore much scripture to the contrary,[23] including the sevenfold challenge of Revelation: "To him that overcometh . . . " But perhaps the best and most graphic argument of all against that idea is David's simple reference to snow.

Snow melts and flows downward through a little mountain stream, and soon it carries an accumulating load of waste. It passes through cities, turning green and then brown. At last it is unfit even for fish to live in, and it arrives at the lowest point on earth, a five-mile-deep ocean.

Now, however, a miracle takes place. God's sun—and you can spell that "Son" if you like—shines on the polluted sea. Tons of water do the impossible, defying gravity and seeking the freedom of the sky. Fluffy cumulus clouds arrive once again over the mountains where all this began. What is it that drifts downward onto the mountainside? Is it pure, white snow? Or polluted seawater *declared* to be snow?

David said it with simple elegance: "Wash me, and I shall be whiter than snow" (Ps. 51:7). From the context it is obvious that he was asking not for excuses but for victory. "Create in me a pure heart, O God, and renew a steadfast spirit within me" (verse 10, N.I.V.). For that kind of faith God could reserve His sincerest praise, referring to him as " ' "my servant David, who kept my commands and followed me with all his heart, doing only what was right in my eyes," ' " (1 Kings 14:8, N.I.V.).

"We would see Jesus." That was the world's request of Christianity. Yet Satan had succeeded in depriving the world of that view by selling many

Christians a counterfeit "gospel" that demanded of the Lord His immortality but not His victorious life. Perhaps alone among all the religions of the world, Christianity sometimes suggested the existence of a God who would save man by lowering His standard. If that were true, the survival of rebellion was guaranteed. For God's standard was perfect, and how do you alter perfection? The answer, of course, is that you do not. In trying, you only create imperfection—and that was what Lucifer had introduced in the beginning.

Perhaps some Christian theologians could not see that, but Chief Joseph understood it when he described with a sickened heart "all the good words and all the broken promises."

That had been the tragedy of Christian theology.

That had been Lucifer's triumph.

And now Adventism was stripping away the façade behind which that error lurked. Instead of the tyranny of self, one could have a beautiful absolute called the law of God, a transcript of the character of Christ. And it was available to anyone through the simple process of faith and surrender.[24]

"We would see Jesus." Now there was a possibility that that message would be delivered. And in the supreme command of the forces of darkness there would be an urgent meeting to discuss how this new movement could be destroyed.

The result would be the enemy battle plan we read of in the first chapter.

[1] Matthew 26; *The Desire of Ages*, pp. 642-651.
[2] Matt. 22:15-22; *The Desire of Ages*, pp. 601-603.
[3] Matthew 27; *The Desire of Ages*, pp. 537-542; 723-764.
[4] John 12:20-43; *The Desire of Ages*, pp. 621-626.
[5] *Testimonies to Ministers*, p. 416; *Testimonies*, vol. 2, pp. 631-677; vol. 4, pp. 562-564.

DECISION AT THE JORDAN

[6] *Christ's Object Lessons*, pp. 69, 329-333; Matt. 7:13-23; *Testimonies*, vol. 6, pp. 369-379.
[7] In an interview with Chief Joseph, "An Indian's Views of Indian Affairs," *North American Review*, April, 1879, p. 432. Also in Helen A. Howard, *War Chief Joseph* (Caldwell, Idaho: Caxton Printers, 1941), p. 297.
[8] *The Great Controversy*, pp. 423-432.
[9] *Ibid.*, pp. 433-438.
[10] *Selected Messages*, book 1, p. 347.
[11] *The Great Controversy*, p. 472; Prov. 28:9; Isa. 59:2; Heb. 6:1-6.
[12] Rev. 12:17; 19:10; Eph. 4:11-15; Amos 3:7.
[13] Rom. 8:1-11.
[14] 1 John 5:3.
[15] Rev. 14:6-15.
[16] *Early Writings*, p. 19.
[17] *Education*, p. 18.
[18] *Christ's Object Lessons*, p. 419.
[19] 1 Cor. 4:9; *Testimonies*, vol. 5, p. 526.
[20] Eph. 2:10; 4:24; Eze. 36:26.
[21] 2 Cor. 5:17.
[22] Matt. 13:46; *Christ's Object Lessons*, pp. 116, 117.
[23] 1 Cor. 9:25-27; 6:9-11; *The Acts of the Apostles*, p. 559.
[24] Gal. 2:20.

4

The Hour of His Judgment

Once again it was autumn.
Across the folded landscape of New England, radiant in autumn's waning sunlight, patches of color still hung on the hillsides: red and yellow and burgundy, summer's hues hoarded by a land that would soon feel winter's wind. This was the waiting time, an interlude when crops were in and pumpkins glowed amid the remnants of last season's corn, when people were inclined to keep indoors and children waited impatiently for the first sign of snow. Yet here and there across New England lonely farm families could be seen working in their fields, bringing in crops that they had not expected to harvest. They were Adventists. They had dared to challenge the world with the prospect of actually

seeing Jesus. Now, their hope deferred, they were returning to the chores they thought they'd never do again.

The Lord had not come.

Once again, it was time to face the tasks of autumn.

And for some reason, most of the professed Christian world was enormously relieved.

Relieved, perhaps, but not rid of Adventism. The world had not heard the last from this little group of people who had dared to tell them that the Lord was coming—people drawn from various denominations, bound together only by their love for truth and their longing to see Jesus. In the autumn of 1844 a small group of Adventists returned to their Bibles with new intensity, seeking a better understanding of the prophecies of Daniel.[1] In the course of their research something happened that is still remarkable, particularly to a person trained in law. Probably none of them had any legal training. Yet they uncovered the judicial process underlying the whole plan of salvation.

One of the unique concepts of Adventism is that of the investigative judgment, beginning in 1844. Drawing on the rich symbolism of the Hebrew sanctuary service, it ties Old and New Testaments together and provides some of our deepest insights into the nature of sin, the mechanism of salvation, and the work of Christ. And in so doing, it puts the whole plan of salvation on a rational legal footing.

In illustrating salvation through the symbolism of the sanctuary, God showed the gospel way of forgiveness through the merits of a substitute. In every sacrifice Israel was to see foreshadowed the coming "Lamb of God" who would take away "the sin of the world" (John 1:29). People were—and are—forgiven and accepted on the basis of their faith in the Redeemer.

But in those services God also revealed to Israel some of the profoundest principles of law. It is legally clear that every wrong deed sets in motion a train of circumstances that often go out of control. Like the small force that dislodges the avalanche, a mistake can produce tragically enduring effects. God Himself warned that sin's results could reach to the "third and fourth generation," thus pointing out a legal truth often overlooked by Christian theologians: there is a great distinction between forgiving sin and dealing with its natural consequences. To put it another way, the effect of sin does not disappear simply because of forgiveness, any more than a mother's prize vase reassembles itself after she forgives her clumsy toddler. The act may be forgiven, but the consequences live on. Sin has to be borne by someone. And only in a day of final judgment will the universe be able to witness the enormity and vast consequences of sin. Such a view would cause even devils to acknowledge God's rightness. "As I live, saith the Lord, every knee shall bow to me, and every tongue shall confess to God" (Rom. 14:11).

A further truth is illustrated in the sanctuary services. Each day people in Israel came to the door of the courtyard seeking forgiveness. There they offered their sin offerings, and the officiating priest mediated the blood by sprinkling it upon the altar of burnt offering and eating a portion of its flesh; in certain instances he sprinkled the blood upon the inner veil. Thus, figuratively, God's people were forgiven and their guilt was transferred to the sanctuary. Day by day the sanctuary assumed, for the time being, the sinner's accountability. But is the Godhead really responsible for sin?

That question was answered on the Day of Atonement. The year's burden of guilt was symbolically removed from the sanctuary and placed on the head of a goat that represented Satan. Foreshadowing his final banishment and destruction, the goat was then led far away from God's people. The sanctuary was said to be "cleansed."[2]

Cleansed. It meant more than forgiveness. It also foretold removing the very record of sin. It meant that one day the divine government, in the presence of a witnessing universe, would formally be cleared of Satan's charges that it was responsible for the sin problem. Satan would stand revealed as the arch rebel, the author of sin. It meant that one day God would send both sin and its effects out with Lucifer into final destruction. And the universe would give their unanimous consent.

The Day of Atonement was also a summons to repentance. And anyone who did not prepare for it by confessing and forsaking sin was banished from the company of God's people.[3]

Thus, most clearly, Israel's Day of Atonement foreshadowed final judgment.[4]

For the pioneers of Adventism, earnestly studying in the years following 1844, this exciting truth broke through like sunshine after a storm. The 2300-day prophecy of Daniel was indeed correct! Something of significance *had* happened on October 22. Judgment had begun![5]

THE HOUR OF HIS JUDGMENT

Eighteen centuries earlier, on a lonely Sabbath at Patmos, Christ had given John messages for seven Christian congregations in Asia. Those messages had deep significance also for coming eras of the Christian church. One of them was sent to the church called Philadelphia, representing a period in the early 1800s, ending about 1844.[6] To this era of His church, the Lord gave a message describing doors and keys, pillars and temples—filled with the very symbols that would be meaningful to people who were about to rediscover God's sanctuary, its apartments, and the mysteriously significant doors that led from one to the next.

" 'To the angel of the church in Philadelphia write: These are the words of him who is holy and true, who holds the key of David. What he opens, no one can shut; and what he shuts, no one can open. I know your deeds. See, I have placed before you an open door that no one can shut. . . . I am coming soon. Hold on to what you have, so that no one can take your crown. Him who overcomes I will make a pillar in the temple of my God' " (Rev. 3:7-12, N.I.V.).[7]

" *'I have placed before you an open door.'* " In 1844, Adventism stood poised at its threshold, soon by faith to view a scene that stretches language: a great radiant throne, over which rested the awesome light, encircled by a rainbow and issuing an endless stream of fire, millions upon millions of angels standing by, a hushed sense of life and death in the air, and in the courtroom, visible by all, heaven's records.[8]

Nearly 2,400 years earlier the prophet Daniel had foreseen this moment and had described it in words that bend the imagination: "'As I looked, thrones were set in place, and the Ancient of Days took his seat. His clothing was as white as snow; the hair of his head was white like wool. His throne was flaming with fire, and its wheels were all ablaze. A river of fire was flowing, coming out from before him. Thousands upon thousands attended him; ten thousand times ten thousand stood before him. *The court was seated, and the books were opened'* " (Dan. 7:9, 10, N.I.V.).

In other words, judgment.

From the dawn of human history, people had known that one day this would come. Daniel foresaw judgment and described its majesty. Paul warned of a "day" when God would judge the world (Acts 17:31). John foretold an "hour" (Rev. 14:7). In Ecclesiastes, the magnificent logic of Solomon had carried the human mind the next step further in an orderly process of reason. If there were to be judgment, there would also have to be an objective, preexisting standard by which one would be judged. "Fear God and keep his commandments, for this is the whole duty of man. For God will bring every deed into judgment, including every hidden thing, whether it is good or evil" (Eccl. 12:13, 14, N.I.V.).

By the year 1857, the pioneers of Adventism had developed an understanding of judgment unprecedented in modern Christianity, and they offered the world a new term, coined to describe what was already under way in heaven: *investigative judgment*. For generations theologians had grappled with the concept of judgment, struggling to understand its meaning, its operation, and its timing. Now a small

THE HOUR OF HIS JUDGMENT

group of Bible students who called themselves Adventists were telling the world's scholars that this event had begun. And the key to understanding judgment, they asserted, lay in understanding the symbolism God Himself had used to illustrate it. That symbolism was found in the Hebrew sanctuary service, where the Day of Atonement perfectly illustrated what had begun in heaven on October 22, 1844. Like the high priest of old (who only typified Christ's present ministry), Jesus Himself was now ministering in the Most Holy Place, reviewing the lives of His professed people; separating the false from the genuine; and—for His true followers—removing the record of their forgiven sins from the books of heaven.

If one stopped to think about it, Adventists had thus happened onto one of the most vital and useful commodities imaginable: a final, absolute answer to the problem of guilt.[9] But there was another exciting implication to their discovery. Probably without realizing it, they had also discovered the legal principles by which God deals with sin and salvation.

People quite frequently come to court requesting something to which they have a right, but which cannot be given them until some future time. Perhaps the best-known illustration in Western law is divorce. Someone appears at court who, under the law, at least, is entitled to a divorce. Yet there is also a strong public need to preserve marriage and encourage reconciliation. Therefore many States require a waiting period, during which time the individual might have a change of mind. Only after that period ends is one entitled to return to court and receive a final divorce decree.

Thus the law appears to be in a state of contradiction. On the one hand, it tells an aggrieved wife that she is absolutely entitled to be single again. On the other, she must wait before she can have the divorce to which she has a right. Why? Because the law recognizes a variable called human nature. People can, and do, change their minds, and the law has to be sure that before final judgment is entered, the person has made a firm decision.

Now the judge faces a dilemma. Before the court stands a person legally entitled to something that cannot yet be granted, a person who wants full assurance regarding her rights yet who may also have a change of mind before final judgment is entered. How does the judge handle the problem? By issuing something called an interlocutory judgment. It simply says that a person is entitled to something that will take place in the future—unless, in the meantime, he or she has a change of mind. The individual has a valid, legal right, and the outcome hinges entirely upon his or her own actions and decisions.

This illustration from modern law can help us understand the mechanism of the plan of salvation. When human beings come to God in the name of Jesus and ask for eternal life, they are requesting something to which they have an absolute legal right, fully purchased at Calvary.[10] At the very moment of belief an individual has the right to live forever in the presence of God.[11] Eternity itself opens. "He that hath the Son hath life" (1 John 5:12)—*hath*, present tense. There can be no better statement of full assurance.

THE HOUR OF HIS JUDGMENT

But is that gift of life irrevocable, or is it contingent? To put it another way, by believing in Jesus does one thereby lose the freedom to change one's mind? Evidently not; a great army of backsliders makes that point all too evident. The gift of eternal life is bestowed with the condition of accepting Christ—with all that this implies, including accepting Him as a living part of one's own life.[12] The relationship is more than a one-time contact;[13] it is an ongoing connection, and to lose it brings tragic consequences. " ' "The righteousness of the righteous man will not save him when he disobeys," ' " Ezekiel wrote. " ' "The righteous man, if he sins, will not be allowed to live because of his former righteousness" ' " (chap. 33:12, N.I.V.). Paul openly expressed concern that even he, who had preached to others, might be a "castaway" (1 Cor 9:27). While belief in Christ calls into being the legal right to live forever, that gift cannot be granted irrevocably until there is no possibility that a person will change his mind and return to sin. For all but a magnificent few, only death has been powerful enough to guarantee that.[14]

Thus the plan of salvation encounters the same problem faced so frequently in earthly courts: how do you grant people something to which they are entitled, but that they may later lose? God is confronted by persons stating a request that He cannot deny—eternal life in the name of Jesus. But He is also dealing with human beings, whose freedom of choice gives them the ability to change their minds. In His wisdom, God does the obvious: He grants an interlocutory judgment.[15]

The conclusion is logically inescapable. The

book of life is a record filled with interlocutory judgments.[16] And that fact alone guarantees that even the redeemed will have their day in court.

That was the issue spoken to with exceptional clarity by Adventism. For generations theologians had argued over the matter of judgment for the righteous, sometimes wondering whether it was even necessary for an all-knowing God to determine who were His and who were not. Confusion on this point had led to confusion on others. To be sure, *probation* closed at death. But some felt that *judgment* also came at death. If so, it was almost inescapable that at death the soul went either to heaven or to hell. Others, puzzled as to how salvation could be assured to people who might later change their minds, solved the problem with the convenient theory that once a person accepted Christ, he was forever saved. Still others, John Calvin and Martin Luther among them, avoided the issue by saying that God had simply predestined some people for salvation—a comfortable solution for theoreticians, perhaps, but precious little comfort to the poor souls who spent their lives in an agony of suspense about whether they were among the "elect." All this in lieu of a simple, magnificently logical legal mechanism now described by Adventism under the term *investigative judgment*.

What Adventism describes makes excellent sense in law; in fact, it is the only theological explanation of judgment that does make sense in a legal setting. Christ was reviewing the records of every person throughout history who had ever had an interlocutory judgment for eternal life. Before the onlooking universe, God was determining

THE HOUR OF HIS JUDGMENT

whether those who once claimed salvation were still requesting it at the end of their probation—and thus whether it was possible to enter final judgment in their favor. And through those who had maintained their relationship with Christ He was demonstrating to all creation that the redeemed had, under the most demanding circumstances in a world of sin, made irrevocable decisions of loyalty to God. The hour of His judgment had come, and Jesus was calling His witnesses.

Almost immediately Adventism came under intense attack. For one thing, some critics said, this whole business about an investigative judgment was utterly unnecessary. Christ had completed His work at Calvary, they declared. There was nothing for man to do but believe that, and any mention of a present day of atonement was an attempt to take Christianity back to Judaism. For these critics Adventism reserved some of its most persuasive logic.

If these people really meant what they were saying, then a person could obtain salvation merely by a single act of "belief," and become irrevocably "saved," regardless of subsequent conduct. Did salvation therefore open the door for continued wrong doing in the name of "freedom"?

There simply was no sensible alternative to Adventism's contention that Calvary, as awesome as it was, did not complete the plan of salvation. Christ's death made salvation legally *possible;* application of that right awaited human response.[17]

For the Christian world, that sort of declaration was—and is—an astonishing mouthful. People conditioned to believe that nothing remained to be done after Calvary were suddenly jolted by an idea that challenged their comfortable preconceptions. Yet if one thought it through, the idea was both scriptural and logical. And it perfectly fit the symbolism of the Jewish sanctuary service. The sanctuary indeed showed that there is a difference between sacrifice and application of its benefits—between slaying the sin offering, typifying Calvary, and the priest's mediation, typifying Christ's work in heaven.[18] And those who liked to say that Christ's work was entirely complete at Calvary were missing a subtle legal point: His death did not impose salvation on people against their will. In a legal sense, it was simply the purchase of their right to eternal life.[19] The exercise of that privilege remained a function of the human will.[20]

To put it in the terminology of contract law, Christ's death was an offer. Before there could be a contractual covenant, there had to be an acceptance of that offer. And that could come only from each individual human heart.[21]

Perhaps there was a reason why some had failed to see this. It was really a question of law—contract law, made possible because of God's mercy.[22] And to understand it, one had to understand the divine law upon which it was based.

Thus Adventism has emphasized a qualification of the term "complete atonement." Adventism recognizes that Christ was fully God, that He lived a sinless life, that He died a vicarious death and fully paid the penalty for man's sins.

But Adventism teaches that in its fullest sense the "complete atonement" does not end with the cross, any more than in the Mosaic type did the

THE HOUR OF HIS JUDGMENT

atonement end with the slaying of the Lord's goat. The blood of the goat had to be carried by the high priest into the sanctuary and there applied against the sins of the people that had accumulated there, symbolically, throughout the year. If there was anyone in the camp who did not participate in the coverage, that person was "cut off" from the people.

Similarly in antitype, as the book of Hebrews explains, Christ as our High Priest carried the efficacy of His sacrifice into the heavenly sanctuary. There, as we request the application of His sacrifice to us personally, the work He did at Calvary is made effective to us today.

And that is not all. The Hebraic Day of Atonement did not end until the scapegoat was taken into the wilderness. So in its fullest sense, Christ's work of atonement is complete when the last vestige of sin is destroyed.

Hiding just beneath the surface of Adventism's sanctuary discovery was a point of law that gives the deepest insights into the nature of sin. In the investigative judgment Christ was determining who would receive final judgments for eternal life. For those who did, He would remove from the books of heaven every trace of the records of their sins.[23] But sin, as so clearly illustrated in the Hebrew services, does not disappear. Sin is a hitchhiker from the realm of death, yearning to go home but unable to get there unless it is attached to some living being. Sin, we are told, is the transgression of the law,[24] and the law can only be transgressed through the act of an intelligent mind.[25] Thus, sin will not walk on its own power down into the lake of fire; it will be carried there by someone. That, in the end, is what the story of the scapegoat is all about.[26]

And that explained why sin, even though forgiven, remained on the books of heaven.[27] It *had* to remain there, for one day sin would be carried to destruction, and Christ had provided mankind with two alternatives as to how that might be done. One could accept salvation, or one could reject it, and thus himself carry the responsibility for his sins into the lake of fire.[28]

Thus in the sanctuary Christ's ministry illustrates that the plan of salvation operates upon principles readily recognizable even in human law. As any lawyer knows, there is a large difference between the existence of a legal right and its application—between, if you will, one's right to salvation and one's acceptance of that right. A person might be entitled to inherit a large estate, yet lose it completely by failing to ask that the will be probated.

So it is with the plan of salvation. Christ on Calvary purchased for every human being the right to have eternal life.[29] Yet even that great gift lay waiting for individual acceptance.[30] For salvation operates by a rule God Himself adopted in the morning of Creation, when He filled the universe with beings to whom He gave the power of free choice.[31] He would not change that plan, even if it meant sending His Son to a cross.[32]

Nor will He change it now. Every person is legally entitled to live forever in God's presence, but only a comparative few will ever realize that joy.[33] Only those who decide to respond to truth. *Only those who ask for cleansing from sin.*[34]

THE HOUR OF HIS JUDGMENT

And there are tragically few on earth who understand what Jesus is doing in heaven. Through one of his most brilliant tactical maneuvers the great enemy has robbed mankind of that truth. He has counterfeited the sanctuary ministry of Christ and sold variations of that counterfeit to nearly all of Christendom.

In the early morning of Christianity, Paul had warned of a mysterious "secret power of lawlessness" that was "already at work" within the church. A man of sin would arise who "even sets himself up in God's temple, proclaiming himself to be God" (2 Thess. 2:3, 4, 7, N.I.V.).

Daniel, too, had warned of a power that "magnified himself even to the prince of the host," and by that power the place of God's sanctuary would be "cast down" (Dan. 8:11). The very essence of the gospel is that man's salvation comes through "one mediator between God and men, the man Christ Jesus" (1 Tim. 2:5), yet both Paul and Daniel describe a power that would interfere in this process, somehow intruding into the very sanctuary ministry of Christ. The genius of primitive Christianity would be lost, and in its place would be substituted an elaborate human device called priestcraft. Often backed by military might, some human force would attempt to intervene in the process of defining and forgiving sin. Christ's unique and vital sanctuary ministry would be counterfeited.

Thus, Lucifer accomplished one of his most stunning successes against the Christian faith, and he did so by attacking the doctrine of the sanctuary. He had watched helplessly as Christ restored mankind's legal entitlement to heaven, but he understood far better than did humanity that there is a vast difference between legal entitlement and salvation. If Satan could confuse people on that point, he could still cost the souls of millions who were now absolutely entitled to eternal life but who could fail to receive it if they did not appropriate that right through continuing surrender to Christ.[35]

The devil also seems quickly to have discovered that by confusing Christians about the work of Christ in the heavenly sanctuary he could confuse them on a whole spectrum of other truths. Coming to depend on a human priesthood, many Christians have lost sight of Christ's continuing role in the plan of salvation. In their homes and churches they are content to portray Him hanging crucified, thus subtly fixating on His death and ignoring His present work for them in heaven. Others believe that His work of salvation was entirely complete at the cross, an appealing idea if one does not thoroughly examine the conclusions to which it could lead: if Christ's work for man *was* absolutely complete at the cross, then one might believe that everyone would have to be saved, for there is nothing left to do. (Most people, if forced to think it through, would have to admit that there is something illogical about forcing Attila the Hun, Nero, and Adolf Hitler into heaven).

In a word, confusion. Lucifer injected error into the concept of the sanctuary—a doctrinal truth many people would not even consider essential for salvation. Yet the results were catastrophic. Christianity began splintering into ever-narrowing schools of theological theory (and ever-widening numbers of Christian sects). Unanswered questions sprouted like mushrooms after a rain. Judgment: when and where would it occur? Not understanding Christ's sanctuary ministry, some scholars solemnly decreed that it would come to each person at death—and hence it seemed inescapable that at death the soul must go either to heaven or hell. Others decided that man must pay a while for his wrongs, and purgatory was the result. Still others solved Lucifer's clever legal problem by adopting other theories: predestination; rapture; second chance; once saved, always saved.

It was, to repeat, a brilliant tactic by Lucifer. Across Christendom learned men argued over problems that did not even exist, while ignoring life-and-death issues that did. In the arguments that followed, civil governments entered the act, and human beings faced the ordeal of religious persecution.[36]

Instead of all this confusion, Adventism offered the investigative judgment—a concept that plumbed the deepest principles of judicial fairness while simultaneously avoiding such problems as the immortality of the soul. It is one of the most innovative concepts in modern theology. *And Adventism rediscovered it!*

Discovered, not invented. Adventist theology did not create these concepts, any more than Newton created gravity, or Bernoulli created the law that lifts three hundred tons of jetliner simply by the motion of air. Great minds have ever acknowledged, with Newton, that they are only rediscovering existing truth, thinking the Creator's thoughts after Him. So it was with a little group of

DECISION AT THE JORDAN

Bible students who mowed hayfields and carried rock on the railroad, and then pooled their meager funds because they thought this stupendous discovery was worth sharing with the world.

Adventism had gone by faith through an open door leading to the very heart of heaven, and had entered a place where John had once seen the "ark of his covenant" (Rev. 11:19, N.I.V). Here awaited a whole system of forgotten truths, each attached to the next with compelling logic, and each recognizable if one understood the graphic symbolism of the Hebrew sanctuary. The law of God. The Sabbath. Judgment. Even a sweeping view of events at the end of human history.[37] If, as Jesus suggested, God's truth can be compared to a miner's hidden treasure, then this—to put it in mining terms—was the glory hole, the place where nuggets lay piled atop one another, the grand prize. This was one of the most exciting discoveries since Pentecost and the Reformation, and it was explored by a little band of praying men and women who began to study just as autumn graced the hillsides of New England with one last splash of golden light—men and women who had entered the Word of God looking for Jesus, and who had discovered that in Him there is an awesome spectrum of wealth.[38]

---

[1] *The Great Controversy*, pp. 403-432; *Special Testimonies*, Series B, No. 2, pp. 56, 57.

[2] Lev. 16:5-22; *Patriarchs and Prophets*, pp. 355-358; *The Great Controversy*, pp. 419-422.

[3] Revelation 20; *The Great Controversy*, pp. 485, 486, 491, 673.

[4] Lev. 23:28-30; *The Great Controversy*, pp. 480, 485-490.

[5] *The Great Controversy*, pp. 423-426.

[6] Rev. 3:7-13

[7] See *The Great Controversy*, p. 435.

[8] Rev. 20:11, 12; Dan. 7:9, 10; 8; 9; *Testimonies*, vol. 2, p. 442; vol. 4, pp. 384-387; vol. 5, p. 59; *The Great Controversy*, pp. 480-487, 666.

[9] Heb. 9:11-15; 10:1-4, 19-23; Isa. 1:18; 65:17; Rev. 21:4; *The Desire of Ages*, pp.

THE HOUR OF HIS JUDGMENT

107, 108, 328-332; *The Acts of the Apostles*, 424, 425; *Testimonies*, vol. 4, p. 395; *The Great Controversy*, pp. 421-432, 485, 619, 620.
    [10] John 3:16.
    [11] Chapter 17.
    [12] Col. 1:24-29; Rom. 12:1, 2; 11:11-24; Phil. 2:1-18; Prov. 28:13; *Steps to Christ*, pp. 57-65; *The Desire of Ages*, pp. 24-26, 555, 556; *The Great Controversy*, pp. 482-491; *Christ's Object Lessons*, pp. 122, 123.
    [13] Ezekiel 33; 2 Peter 1:3-12.
    [14] Rev. 22:11, 12; *The Great Controversy*, pp. 482-491, 603-652.
    [15] Eze. 33:18; 2 Peter 2:6; *The SDA Bible Commentary*, Ellen G. White Comments, on Eph. 1:4, 5, 11, p. 1114; *Testimonies*, vol. 5, pp. 629-635.
    [16] *The Great Controversy*, p. 483.
    [17] *Testimonies*, vol. 5, pp. 513-516, 629-650.
    [18] *The Great Controversy*, pp. 417-422; *Patriarchs and Prophets*, pp. 355-358.
    [19] John 1:12, 13.
    [20] Verses 10-13, N.I.V.; *Testimonies*, vol. 5, pp. 513-516.
    [21] *The Desire of Ages*, pp. 81-83; Isa. 1:19, 20; *The Great Controversy*, pp. 539-543; *Testimonies*, vol. 2, 200-215; vol. 4, pp. 213-221, 387.
    [22] Heb. 10:16.
    [23] *The Great Controversy*, pp. 421, 422, 483.
    [24] 1 John 3:4.
    [25] James 4:17; *Counsels on Diet and Foods*, p. 69.
    [26] Leviticus 16; Revelation 20; *The Great Controversy*, pp. 422, 673; *Patriarchs and Prophets*, pp. 355-358.
    [27] *The Great Controversy*, p. 483.
    [28] *Patriarchs and Prophets*, pp. 355-358; *The Great Controversy*, p. 673.
    [29] John 3:16; 1 Tim. 2:4-6.
    [30] 2 Peter 3:9; Rom. 8:1-14.
    [31] Joshua 24:15; *Education*, p. 23; *Patriarchs and Prophets*, pp. 48, 49.
    [32] Gen. 3:15; *Prophets and Kings*, pp. 701, 702; *The Desire of Ages*, pp. 22-26.
    [33] Matt. 7:13-23.
    [34] Eze. 33:11; 1 John 1:6, 7; 2 Thess. 2:8-13; James 5:19, 20.
    [35] James 4:7; Gal. 5:19-25; 1 Cor. 6:9-11; *Testimonies*, vol. 5, pp. 692, 693; *Steps to Christ*, pp. 57-65.
    [36] Dan. 7:25; Matt. 24:15-23; Rev. 12:5, 6, 14; 13:1-10; *The Great Controversy*, pp. 49-288.
    [37] *The Great Controversy*, pp. 433-460.
    [38] *Special Testimonies*, Series B, No. 2, pp. 56, 57; *The Great Controversy*, pp. 401-422.

5

The Real Shaking of Adventism

It was one hour past midnight. In the cold predawn of a morning in 1904, Ellen White was already up, writing as rapidly as her pen could move across the page. She had just had a dream, the import of which she understood all too clearly, and her words spilled out into a warning still uncomfortably vivid today.

The church of God, she said, was like a ship on a foggy, treacherous ocean, about to hit a huge iceberg head on![1]

How could it have come to this? By all odds God's people should have already been home, safe in the harbor of eternity. Instead, the ship had strayed into that fog-bound corner of the ocean where death lurks hidden in the mist, concealing

THE REAL SHAKING OF ADVENTISM

the greatest portion of its threat beneath the surface. How could a noble vessel, cared for by God Himself, drift so far off course and into such danger?

The answer to that question was remarkably simple: the ship had failed to follow its chart!

For years Ellen White had been pleading with God's people to spread out during these last moments of history's summer, to go to the world when the work would be relatively easy. Instead, many of the brightest and best trained had packed into Battle Creek, turning Adventist institutions into great centers where workers gradually lost their sense of mission. Now the effects of that mistake were beginning to compound. Funds desperately needed in the mission field were instead being hoarded in Battle Creek while institutions grew to several times the size recommended by God. And around these institutions began to coalesce a group of educated, articulate people who found themselves becoming more and more antagonistic to church leadership and to Ellen White.

Now, in the gloomy hours just past midnight, Mrs. White was telling the church that the worst possible result had finally come, a massive crisis in doctrine that could no longer be avoided. The very rationale for Adventism had been challenged right within the church. And the resulting collision would be like a ship hitting an iceberg.

What does that past crisis have to do with a new generation of Adventists, most of whom were not even living when those events took place? Simply this: Ellen White said it would happen again. "Be not deceived," she warned; "many will depart from the faith, giving heed to seducing spirits and doctrines of devils. We have now before us the alpha of this danger. The omega will be of a most startling nature."[2]

Alpha had arrived. Omega would come. And Ellen White "trembled" for our people.

The certainty of a great shaking, in which members will be lost to the cause, is an incongruous and yet inevitable part of Adventism. Somewhere there will be a great challenge in which we can expect to lose even "men of talent and pleasing address."[3] "The time is not far distant when the test will come to every soul," Ellen White once warned. "Many a star that we have admired for its brilliancy will then go out in darkness. Chaff like a cloud will be borne away on the wind, even from places where we see only floors of rich wheat."[4] And in the last great conflict between God's people and the world, their most formidable enemies will be those who have left the Advent message.[5]

How could such a thing happen? How could a system of truth so filled with inspiration and logic lose some of its best-trained minds—either in 1904 or in the crisis called omega? For the answer we must go back nearly six thousand years. Back to Eden. Back to the beginning of the real shaking of Adventism.

It was the morning of history. For some time—history does not tell us how long—Adam and Eve had enjoyed the warmth of creation's springtime. For them life had been God's gift—unearned and undeserved, something simply handed them as an act of love. But like all of God's gifts, it was conditioned on faith. So long as Adam and Eve had

THE REAL SHAKING OF ADVENTISM

faith in God, life would go on endlessly. And to measure their faith, God had created a very simple test. Would they believe something for which He gave them absolutely no sensory confirmation—that an apparently harmless tree, located in the middle of their beautiful Garden, contained an impostor called death?[6]

That confronted Adam and Eve with a broader question. Would they subject God's revealed truth to their own analysis and judgment? Before believing, would they demand that God's word first be validated and reinterpreted by the human mind?

It was a question that needed to be settled once and for all, for there were a thousand ways in which Adam could begin to question God, to use the magnificent power of reason to rebel, as Lucifer had done. Adam could, if he wished, question the whole story of Creation. He was surrounded by mature trees, for example, whose rate of growth could be studied. At some point he could graph that growth rate backward and "prove" that Creation could not possibly have happened in a week. And what about himself? He was a grown man; humanity developed slowly from infancy onward. Scientifically, Adam would one day be able to "prove" from existing data that there was more to the beginning of life than one found in the account God had given.

For a mind like Adam's, endless questions could be asked if he ever decided to trade faith for rebellion. And should that happen, sin would be waiting eagerly to claim him—sin, as described earlier, a hitchhiker from the world of death, whose greatest joy would be to make its grisly homeward

DECISION AT THE JORDAN

trip hooked to human lives.

Those were the issues. Now watch the enemy attack, as he attacks today, by first suggesting doubt about a message from God. " 'Did God really say, "You must not eat from any tree in the garden"?' " (Gen. 3:1, N.I.V.).

It is an approach magnificently tailored to the human mind. There is a possibility, Lucifer suggests, that God did not really say it quite the way you remember it. And your perception of God's statement is in any event colored by your own background and ideas. If God really said what you think He said, He would be a monster trying to deprive you of the growth that is your very birthright. Rethink it, Eve. Reinterpret His words according to later discovered facts. Look, I'm eating the fruit—and did you ever hear a serpent speak before?

Eve is faced with analytical criticism of the word of God—and she is about to go under. Her senses and her logic tell her that Lucifer is right. There is absolutely nothing about the tree to which she can point to argue in God's favor. Against the mighty weapon of logic based on lies, she has utterly nothing to offer except naked faith. Watch now as the Bible portrays in slow motion the first "shaking of Adventism": "When the woman saw that the fruit of the tree was good for food and pleasing to the eye, and also desirable for gaining wisdom, she took some and ate it" (verse 6, N.I.V.). But she didn't stop there. How quickly false doctrine turns people into missionaries, determined to spread error to everyone they meet. Eve's first act was to bring her error home to her husband, who would

THE REAL SHAKING OF ADVENTISM

rather risk death than to risk losing Eve.

And the whole grim nightmare of rebellion crashed down upon the human race: a falling leaf, and animals dying so that Adam and Eve could ward off the strange evening chill, and across the horizon of history the sound of marching armies, and a mother staring numbly at a coffin and a folded flag. All because the human mind could look at "evidence" and "see" that God had not really meant what He said.[7]

And that is the strategy Lucifer will try to use against Adventism. For years we have known that the mysterious and dreaded shaking would involve false doctrine. Clear back in the 1880s we were told that "God will arouse His people; if other means fail, heresies will come in among them, which will sift them, separating the chaff from the wheat."[8] Elsewhere we are told that the shaking comes "by the introduction of false theories," and that those who have not really studied for themselves will be swept away "like shifting sand."[9]

But why does that happen? Why do we lose some of our brightest and best minds? Why do they become our most formidable opponents? I suggest that the answer lies in Eden. They, like Eve, decide to set their own minds up against the revealed will of God. They "reinterpret" the Bible (or the Spirit of Prophecy) by deciding what the prophet "really" meant, given his or her background, social setting, and "community acceptance." And in so doing they open the door for one of the most dangerous of all intruders, the subjective human mind.[10]

Humanity's only hope is an absolute better than itself. Like the man in a well, we are helpless to escape without the power of God—helpless in the darkness even to render an intelligent opinion about our own condition. "The Lord looked down from heaven upon the children of men, to see if there were any that did understand, and seek God," the psalmist wrote, and he hastened to add that "there is none that doeth good, no, not one" (Ps. 14:2, 3). Jeremiah added his thoughts on the subject. "The heart is deceitful above all things, and desperately wicked: who can know it?" (Jer. 17:9). If there is one thing humanity does not need, it is to reduce the Word of God to fallible, subjective human judgment.[11]

Yet some current theological methods produce that very result. The Word of God is analyzed and reinterpreted until it is unrecognizable. Creation becomes a symbol compatible with evolution. The Flood is regarded as only a local event in Mesopotamia, greatly exaggerated by Bible writers, who from their vantage point thought it was larger than it was.[12] And the law of God is called an anachronism, relevant only to an agrarian Hebrew economy.

And that, of course, leaves the door open for what man really wants to accomplish: comfortable coexistence with sin.

If we follow that course in Adventist theology, we will have set in motion a train of circumstances that will lead to skepticism, disbelief in the writings of Ellen White, confusion about such clear Biblical truths as Creation, and an atmosphere in which some consider themselves to be intellectuals at odds with the church. How do we know? Because that general scenario has happened repeatedly in churches that once firmly believed in the Bible but now spiritualize away its plainest truths.

Before the time of Christ, young Jewish rabbis began to attend Hellenistic schools of philosophy in Alexandria. There was great turmoil for a while in Israel over whether this should or should not be. Some of the devout felt that this could mean the destruction of Judaism, producing a subtle mixture of truth and error, masquerading as intellectualism, that would captivate their best young minds and alter the whole future of the Jewish religion. Others argued that their young men would merely witness for the Jewish faith and thus produce converts among the Greeks. Ultimately the liberal faction won out. Judaism exposed itself to Platonic philosophy. And generation after generation of rabbis came home, each more concerned than the last about academic degrees, philosophy, and intellectualism. And events had begun that would continue until a generation of Hebrew scholars could give to visiting "heathen" wise men explicit directions to the site of Christ's birth—while not even perceiving the heralding star over Bethlehem![13]

Contrast that with the simple, magnificent faith of Abraham, to whom God gave directions that made no human sense. He was told to leave home and travel to a country he would never personally own. His descendants would be many years in slavery before possessing it. The instruction made no economic sense. It made no emotional sense. For the rest of his life Abraham would be only a wandering pilgrim, who would even have to negotiate for a tomb in which to bury his wife. There were many reasons why Abraham might very much wish to reinterpret the will of God. The record of his life says simply that he "obeyed."[14]

And thus faithful Abraham learned to know the voice of God so well that he could recognize it even when asked for the sacrifice of his own son. His relationship with God had now grown to a deep, personal friendship; with a friend like Abraham, God could share a little of the pain He would later feel at a place called Calvary.[15]

"Except ye be converted, and become as little children, ye shall not enter into the kingdom of heaven" (Matt. 18:3). Hard language for the proud human mind, perhaps, but there it is, from the Lord Himself. Simple, unquestioning faith was a prerequisite even to conversion, the most basic step in Christian living. There is nothing obscure about language like that, nothing requiring historical analysis to understand it. There is salvation there for the humblest as well as the brightest—salvation even for the deepest student, who is big enough to realize, with Newton, that the greatest mind is like a child's mind, willing to think God's thoughts after Him; humble enough to accept truth, honest enough to obey.[16]

Now compare that with the language of Ellen White, who, foreseeing the aftermath of the tragic shaking, tells us that God's work will be finished by humble people.

"The days are fast approaching when there will be great perplexity and confusion. Satan, clothed in angel robes, will deceive, if possible, the very elect. . . . Every wind of doctrine will be blowing. Those who have rendered supreme homage to 'science falsely so called' will not be the leaders then. Those who have trusted to intellect, genius, or talent will not then stand at the head of the rank and file. . . . In the last solemn work few great men will be engaged."[17]

Lest the implications of all this escape, let us recognize how comprehensive a tragedy is described here. Somewhere in the future of God's people waits an overpowering delusion perfectly capable of deceiving even the brightest and the best. God's work will lose some of the very minds it can least afford to lose, those who could stand as champions for truth in its finest hour.

That is an unthinkable loss, for Adventism has always embraced Bible scholarship. It reveals truth as a magnificent system of logic, worthy of defense by the brightest minds. It desperately needs the brightest and the best.

Yet the servant of the Lord describes a scene that ought to drive everyone—scholars and lay persons alike—to their knees. "Many a star that we have admired for its brilliancy will then go out in darkness. Chaff like a cloud will be borne away on the wind, even from places where we see only floors of rich wheat."[18]

Why? Because even the brightest and best-trained human mind, when it once departs from faith, is subject to the same mistake made by Eve. Probably no mind today begins to approach that of Eve, fresh from the Creator's hand. She walked and talked with God, and learned from plants and trees in Eden the very secrets of their lives.[19] Yet she allowed herself the luxury of subjecting the revealed truth of God to her own data base and reasoning. And she soon learned that the cost of

DECISION AT THE JORDAN

that experiment was infinite.

There may be another reason for the shaking of Adventism. It seems to involve behavior—whether God's people will live for principle rather than for expediency.

"There are few really consecrated men among us, few who have fought and conquered in the battle with self. Real conversion is a decided change of feelings and motives; it is a virtual taking leave of worldly connections . . . a withdrawing from the controlling power of their thoughts, opinions, and influences. *The separation causes pain and bitterness to both parties.*"[20]

What is the great behavioral issue that will cause such polarization? Lucifer himself admitted it. "'The Sabbath is the great question which is to decide the destiny of souls.'"[21] Why? Because it represents the same issue that confronted the human mind in Eden: will we obey, even when we cannot validate God's requirement from human data and reason?

Instead of a tree, mankind will encounter a day of worship. Among the commandments, the Sabbath is unique. All the remaining nine can be validated by human reason; most have even been recognized by earthly governments as desirable standards for human behavior. But the Sabbath does not fit this category. It stands alone. One does not reason to it; it simply exists. To recognize the Sabbath, one has to have absolute faith. And for people who emphasize righteousness by faith, the Sabbath thus becomes a pivotal issue.[22]

Now watch that issue operate, even within Adventism. "Those who have step by step yielded to worldly demands and conformed to worldly customs will not find it a hard matter to yield to the powers that be, rather than to subject themselves to derision, insult, threatened imprisonment, and death."[23]

Yet, prophetlike, Ellen White does not leave us without hope. God's work will go on; His message will survive. "The Lord has faithful servants, who in the shaking, testing time will be disclosed to view." Their message may not be borne with polished perfection; "it may be under a rough and uninviting exterior the pure brightness of a genuine Christian character will be revealed."[24] But in God's estimation they will be the real "stars" at the end of time, for God has always delighted to show what He can do with human beings who are humble enough to let Him work[25]—men like a rough-hewn, converted fisherman who could speak in the Temple and draw three thousand people to decision in a single sermon.[26]

"The deeper the night for God's people, the more brilliant the stars. Satan will sorely harass the faithful; but, in the name of Jesus, they will come off more than conquerors."[27]

And that is the final chapter in the shaking of Adventism.

[1] *Selected Messages*, book 1, p. 205.
[2] *Ibid.*, p. 197.
[3] *The Great Controversy*, p. 608.
[4] *Testimonies*, vol. 5, p. 81.
[5] *The Great Controversy*, p. 608.
[6] Genesis 2; 3.
[7] *Patriarchs and Prophets*, pp. 44-62
[8] *Testimonies*, vol. 5, p. 707.
[9] *Testimonies to Ministers*, p. 112.
[10] *Testimonies*, vol. 5, pp. 93, 94.
[11] *The Ministry of Healing*, pp. 427-438.
[12] 2 Peter 3:3-7.

DECISION AT THE JORDAN

[13] *The Desire of Ages*, pp. 27-67; F. C. Gilbert, "Why the Jews Rejected Jesus as the Messiah," unpublished manuscript.

[14] Heb. 11:8-19; *Patriarchs and Prophets*, pp. 125-131.

[15] *Ibid.*, pp. 145-155.

[16] *The Ministry of Healing*, pp. 427-438; *Testimonies to Ministers*, pp. 419, 420; *The Great Controversy*, pp. 593-602.

[17] *Testimonies*, vol. 5, p. 80.

[18] *Ibid.*, p. 81.

[19] *Education*, p. 21.

[20] *Testimonies*, vol. 5, pp. 82, 83. (Italics supplied.)

[21] *Testimonies to Ministers*, p. 472.

[22] *The SDA Bible Commentary*, Ellen G. White comments, on Ex. 20:8-11, p. 1106.

[23] *Testimonies*, vol. 5, p. 81.

[24] *Ibid.*, pp. 80, 81.

[25] *The Ministry of Healing*, p. 150.

[26] Acts 2.

[27] *Testimonies*, vol. 5, pp. 81, 82.

6

Decision at the Jordan

Once in a while, it happens.

Most of the time our lives are relatively uneventful, calmly moving through a familiar routine. The seasons come and go, the school years pass—first for us, and then for our little ones. Like a river with a deceptively quickening pace, life bears us along, first toward middle age and then away from it.

If in the process we avoid great trials, we usually consider ourselves fortunate. Perhaps in a way we are *un*fortunate, for we have missed the privilege of facing the great challenge—of putting everything on the line for a cause worth dying for.

But once in a while it happens.

From time to time the forces of history converge, bringing people to a moment filled with the raw materials of greatness. And I think that is happening today.

It is happening to Adventism.

And it is time to move quickly.

What I am about to say I could, I suppose, try to phrase in some novel way to capture your imagination. Instead, I am going to say it simply.

I believe we are very near the end.

I believe the enemy has begun the last great offensive of the war.

And I think that constitutes his admission that heaven is now within our grasp.

Listen to the words of inspiration, more meaningful now than when they were penned:

"Savage wolves will come in among you and will not spare the flock. Even from your own number men will arise and distort the truth in order to draw away disciples after them" (Acts 20:29, 30, N.I.V.).

"False theories, clothed with garments of light, will be presented to God's people. Thus Satan will try to deceive, if possible, the very elect. Most seducing influences will be exerted; minds will be hypnotized."[1]

"The very last deception of Satan will be to make of none effect the testimony of the Spirit of God."[2]

Perhaps John Kennedy said it best. "In the long history of the world, only a few generations have been granted the role of defending freedom in its hour of maximum danger."[3] Today we have been granted the role of defending God's truth in this world's hour of maximum danger. From the beginning of time the people of God have looked by faith to this moment, when the flag of truth would go over the top for the last time. *And it has happened*

DECISION AT THE JORDAN

to us! All the pieces are in place. Something is about to happen. Like Israel, we face two great questions. Will we believe God's revealed truth? And will we obey it?

We have reached the Jordan.

And it is time for a decision.

---

[1] *Testimonies*, vol. 8, p. 293.
[2] *Selected Messages*, book 1, p. 48. (Italics supplied.)
[3] Inaugural address, 1961.